You
Know
I Can't Hear You
When the Water's
Running

You
Know
I Can't Hear You
When the Water's
Running

ROBERT ANDERSON

Random House · *New York*

For Audrey Wood

CONTENTS

YOU KNOW I CAN'T HEAR YOU WHEN THE WATER'S RUNNING
was first presented by Jack Farren and Gilbert Cates at the
Ambassador Theatre in New York City on March 13, 1967,
with the following cast:

(IN ORDER OF APPEARANCE)

THE SHOCK OF RECOGNITION
A producer's office

JACK BARNSTABLE	George Grizzard
HERB MILLER	Joe Silver
DOROTHY	Melinda Dillon
RICHARD PAWLING	Martin Balsam

THE FOOTSTEPS OF DOVES
A basement showroom of a bedding store

SALESMAN	George Grizzard
HARRIET	Eileen Heckart
GEORGE	Martin Balsam
JILL	Melinda Dillon

I'LL BE HOME FOR CHRISTMAS
An apartment living room and kitchen

CHUCK	Martin Balsam
EDITH	Eileen Heckart
CLARICE	Melinda Dillon

I'M HERBERT
A side porch

HERBERT	George Grizzard
MURIEL	Eileen Heckart

Directed by Alan Schneider
Scenery designed by Ed Wittstein
Costumes designed by Theoni V. Aldredge
Lighting designed by Jules Fisher

The Shock of Recognition

The action takes place in the office of a producer. There are doors to the left and right.

JACK BARNSTABLE, *the playwright—slight and intellectual —is waiting. In a moment,* HERB MILLER, *the producer, enters through the door right in a hurry. He is large, a rough diamond. He smokes a cigar.*

HERB Sorry to keep you waiting, Jack. How are you?
(*They shake hands warmly*)

JACK I'm fine, Herb.

HERB Good trip?

JACK Great.

HERB I'm damned excited about producing this play of yours.
(*He picks up a manuscript and waves it*)

JACK Good.

HERB Did you order coffee? The girl can get you coffee.

JACK No, thanks. I just finished breakfast.

HERB (*Snaps on the intercom on his desk*) Dorothy?

DOROTHY (*Her voice is heard*) Yes, Mr. Miller?

HERB Any calls?

DOROTHY No, Mr. Miller.

HERB I don't want to be disturbed.

DOROTHY Yes, Mr. Miller . . .

HERB (*Sits at the desk*) Now, Jack . . . I've been talking to that agent of yours, and he says you mean it when you say in your script here . . . (*He reads*) "Patrick, age forty-three, enters from the bathroom naked."

JACK Well, sure. It's in the script.

HERB I know. But I thought maybe it was there just to give an indication for the actor or director.

JACK No. I mean it.

HERB Well, Jack . . . I mean, hell! You've written a lot of plays. You know we can't do that.

JACK Why not?

HERB We'd be put in jail. You'd offend people.

JACK Why should people be offended by a naked man?

HERB Oh, come on . . .

JACK Damn it, Herb, it's about time our theatre grew up . . . We got to let some air in here someplace . . . It's not as though I were trying to do something sexy. Far from it . . . Look, when Ibsen put a real-life scene on the stage in 1889, the audience recognized their own lives and stood up and cheered.

HERB Well, if you put a naked man onstage, they're gonna stand up and go home.

JACK I'm not asking you to show a couple making love on-stage.

HERB That'll come next.

JACK I just want the audience to get that shock of recognition . . . to feel at home . . . to say, "My God, that's just like us." Look, the wife's lying there in bed reading

4

the morning newspapers . . . (HERB *suddenly looks at the script frantically*) What's the matter?

HERB   I just thought I'd better check. Is she naked too?

JACK   No, Herb. For God's sake! She's lying there. She can be dressed six layers deep, as far as I'm concerned . . . and she's reading the papers and chattering away to her husband, who is in the bathroom . . . water running. Suddenly the water is turned off. Husband appears in the bedroom, . . . with toothbrush in his hand, naked, and says, "Honey, you know I can't hear you when the water's running." He stands there a moment . . .

HERB   Just long enough for everyone to faint.

JACK   . . . goes back in, and the next time we see him, he has a robe on, and that's that.

HERB   Why?

JACK   I told you. The shock of recognition. For the same reason they put running water onstage in *The Voice of the Turtle.*

HERB   Jack, baby, that was twenty-five years or more ago. We're in a different kind of theatre now.

JACK   Okay . . . I'll release you from your contract. What the hell . . .

HERB   Wait a minute, Jack . . .

JACK   It's important to me, Herb. This is not a sexy, muscular man . . . bare to the waist and full of erotic implications as to what he's got in his bulging blue jeans. I want to show man as he is . . . you . . . me . . .

HERB   Speak for yourself . . .

JACK   . . . what Shakespeare called a poor forked radish

5

. . . with no implications except of mortality and ridiculousness.

HERB You find a naked man ridiculous?

JACK Mostly, yes. And so do you. I think the males in the audience will howl with delight and recognition.

HERB At seeing this guy flapping in the breeze?

JACK Yeah. A real man, naked. And, of course, in the play he's quite a guy. He's our hero.

HERB (*Looking at the script*) You know, you didn't say in the script that not only do you want a naked man . . . you want a ridiculous-looking naked man.

JACK That's the whole point. I don't want an Adonis onstage. That's what the movies and the other boys are getting at, the thing I'm trying to get away from.

HERB (*Reads*) "He is touching in his nakedness . . ." Do you find a naked man "touching"?

JACK Well . . . actually that was Sarah's expression. She finds a naked man . . . especially his rear end . . . "touching." When she said it, she called my attention to it, I took a look in the mirror.

HERB And did you find your . . . tail . . . touching?

JACK Look—

HERB I think it's Sarah needs the analyst, not you. "Touching." Sounds kind of maternal, as though she wanted to use some baby powder on it . . . The last time I looked, I didn't find my behind touching . . . Nor does Gloria. She just finds it big . . . Mr. Big-Ass she calls me, if you'll excuse the expression. And I say, "Honey, you can't drive a spike with a tack hammer." Now, that's our relationship. Yours is obviously something else again.

6

JACK   Look, Herb—

HERB   Wait a minute, now. Let me suggest a compromise. If it's the rear end that's so touching, I mean . . . maybe we could get away with just showing that. They did that in *Marat-Sade* and got away with it.

JACK   No.

HERB   You want the whole works?

JACK   Yes.

HERB   I hesitate to ask you how your wife characterizes your . . . uh . . . your . . . Does she find that touching, too?

JACK   She finds it no work of art . . . nor does any woman, as I understand it, though I haven't done a house-to-house poll on it. It's the boys who find it a work of stunning magnificence . . . And I want to blast that. I want every man in the audience to want to reach out and shake my hand.

HERB   And every woman to reach out and pat your fanny.

JACK   I knew you'd give me a fight on this, Herb . . . so I brought some pictures.

HERB   (*Starts for the door, left*)   Should I lock the door?

JACK   Come on now, look. (*He takes two pictures from a briefcase*) Now that's what we're used to seeing . . . the idealized image of a naked man . . . fantasy! This is a normal, real man, naked.

HERB   (*Winces at the second picture*)   I may be queer, but I like the first one better . . . Look upon this, dear mother . . . and on this . . . where the hell did you ever find a guy looked that pathetic? It's not you, is it? (*He steps back and looks*) You take these pictures?

7

JACK No.

HERB I tell you what I think . . . I think the men are not going to reach out and shake your hand. They're gonna want to reach out and belt you one for showing up how ridiculous they are. Because no matter what your wife thinks, I don't think any man feels that his . . . thing . . . is ridiculous. I think he feels it's a formidable weapon, an awesome . . . thing.

JACK Is that the way you think of it, something to attack with . . . aggressive . . . battering?

HERB Well, I don't think of it as ridiculous.

JACK I wonder what Gloria thinks of it.

HERB I'm not going to ask her.

JACK No. I wouldn't take the chance.

HERB You know, Jack, I had Hank in mind for this part.

JACK I think he'd be great.

HERB You don't foresee any obstacle? Any eensy, weensy, ridiculous, pathetic obstacle?

JACK How do you know that Hank wouldn't think it about time—

HERB That someone saw him naked onstage? Somehow I don't think it's ever entered his mind. It's you who have this compulsion to exhibit yourself via some poor actor bastard . . . before the admiring public.

JACK I don't want them to admire.

HERB You want them to laugh. What masochism!

JACK Okay, we'll get some unknown who'll leap at the chance to play a part like this.

8

HERB I'm afraid if he leaps at the chance to appear naked on the stage, he's exactly the kind you don't want.

JACK Well, somebody . . . My God.

HERB I think an unknown would be ill-advised to do it, even for the chance to play the lead in a play of yours. Can't you see him for the rest of his career. Supposing he goes on to play Shakespeare, Hamlet, Lear, Oedipus. Nobody will ever be able to wipe out that touching image of him standing there naked with his toothbrush in his hand, saying, "Honey, you know I can't hear you when the water's running."

JACK Look, Herb, haven't I earned the right to ask for this? The public knows me as a serious playwright . . . not someone just out for kicks and shocks. And if I feel that it's an important step forward in my playwriting, for all playwrights . . . I mean, are we going to let all the daring things be done in the wrong name because we're scared?

HERB Jack, old friend, you have a fine play here. It's that rare combination . . . the public will love it, and the intellectuals won't be too contemptuous.

JACK Why the hell should we in the theatre be so far behind the times? Have you read a book recently . . . what they put in books? Or seen a movie?

HERB Look, it's already hard enough putting on a serious play this day and age. People say, "I got enough troubles in my life. Why come to the theatre to see the same thing?" Now you'll have them saying, "Look, I see my poor, pathetic, ridiculous husband walking around naked all the time. I don't want to come to the theatre to see another ridiculous naked man I don't even know."

JACK (*Vehemently*) I want to say to that plain, ordinary man, her husband, I want to say to him in the audience . . . "Hello. We haven't forgotten you."

HERB And he'll call back and say, "I wish the hell you would."

JACK I want to say, "Hello. You're sick of seeing bizarre, way-out problems of men who aren't men and women who aren't women. Here you are!"

HERB This is your life! Right down to your bare ass and pathetic—

JACK Herb, you don't want to do this play?
      (*He heads for his overcoat and starts to put it on*)

HERB Take it easy. Have you thought of the . . . uh . . . problem of casting . . . of auditioning for this part if Hank doesn't play it? I mean, actors are used to being turned down because they're too short or too tall. But to be turned down because their equipment is not ridiculous enough.

JACK You're so damned prudish, you won't even call it by its right name . . . all these euphemisms . . . Equipment . . . Thing . . .

HERB What would you like me to call it?

JACK The technical word . . . the correct word . . . is penis.

HERB If you go around calling it that, I understand why you think of it as pathetic and ridiculous. It's a ridiculous and belittling name. You call it what you want to call it, and I'll call it what I want to call it. But I've got to tell you something . . . I called it what I did partly because of you.

JACK What do you mean?

HERB All the years I've known you, I still find myself apologizing when I use a dirty word in front of you.

JACK Oh, come on.

HERB   It's the truth. There's something about you. I always find myself saying "Sorry" . . . "Excuse it" . . . And that's another reason I think you're wrong to do this. The public doesn't see you as that kind of writer.

JACK   I'm sorry as hell I've been inhibiting you all these years, Herb. That's one of the most insulting things anyone has ever said to me.

HERB   I can't help it. It's true. Just something about you.

JACK   Would you care to explain that?

HERB   (*At the intercom*) Dorothy?

DOROTHY   (*On the intercom*) Yes, Mr. Miller.

HERB   Will you step in a minute? (*To* JACK) You met her, didn't you?

JACK   (*Puzzled as to what this is all about*) When I came in, yes.

HERB   She's a Bennington girl doing her three months' stint of learning about real life.
(DOROTHY *enters*)

HERB   Dorothy, you know Mr. Barnstable . . . (*To* JACK) She's a great fan of yours. (DOROTHY *is embarrassed*) She played in one of your plays at college.

DOROTHY   Oh, Mr. Miller. Really!

JACK   (*Trying to be pleasant*) Which one?

DOROTHY   Oh, I was terrible!

JACK   I'm sure you weren't.

DOROTHY   (*Insistent*) I was! I was just horrible!

JACK   What part?

11

DOROTHY   If I told you, you'd drop dead right on the spot. Just awful!

HERB   Dorothy, tell me something. You read Mr. Barnstable's play?

DOROTHY   Yes.

HERB   You liked it?

DOROTHY   (*Beams on* JACK)   Oh, yes, I did.

HERB   You read the stage directions?

DOROTHY   Well . . . yes.

HERB   The one in the beginning where the man comes out of the bathroom naked . . . You see, she's blushing just from my reading the stage directions.

DOROTHY   I wasn't blushing.

HERB   You were. Mr. Barnstable here has the idea he actually wants the man to come out naked in that scene . . . (DOROTHY *giggles*) You see, deeper blushes.

DOROTHY   (*Giggling and angry*)   I'm *not* blushing.

HERB   Now here's a broad-minded educated girl . . . Her mind accepts the idea, but her soul blushes.

DOROTHY   (*Put out*)   Oh, Mr. Miller. I'm not blushing.

HERB   Okay. Would you like to pay your six-ninety to see a naked man onstage?

DOROTHY   (*Confused, she giggles*)   It's not a fair question.

HERB   Why not?

DOROTHY   Well, it just isn't.

HERB   Sounds like you got some kind of conflict going there.

12

You would like to see him, but you don't want to admit it.

DOROTHY   Oh, no.

HERB   Do women get a boot out of seeing naked men?

DOROTHY   Oh, Mr. Miller.

HERB   Do they or don't they? (DOROTHY *squirms*) Do you
. . . or don't you?

DOROTHY   Mr. Miller!
   (*She heads for the door, left*)

HERB (*To* JACK)   She's an incompetent witness. She's never
seen a naked man.

DOROTHY (*Stops*)   Mr. Miller!

HERB   Oh, then you have?

DOROTHY   You certainly don't expect a person to answer that.

HERB   All right, go out and pull yourself together . . . I just
wanted to demonstrate to our playwright here what even
the idea of a naked man does to you.

DOROTHY   That's not fair.

HERB   There go your matinées . . .

JACK   Nonsense. I gave this to my grandmother to read,
and her only comment was, "Let me know when it opens
and I'll be there with my opera glasses." . . . Women are
bored with this respectability which red-blooded but prudish
men have forced on them . . . They want to be let in on
the joke.

HERB   Dorothy, do you find a man's sexual equipment ridiculous and pathetic?

DOROTHY   Mr. Miller!
   (*She runs out gasping and in confusion*)

HERB Do you think she meant "yes" or "no"?

JACK You're a cruel bastard. That's a cheap way of getting your kicks.

HERB She's kind of cute, isn't she?

JACK Getting yourself all worked up, talking about the great Forbidden. That's what I'm driving at.

HERB I'm sorry if I didn't keep it on a high intellectual plane . . . But people just aren't going to. A baby . . . a naked male boy, age two . . . they'll goo-goo over, blush a little and say "Isn't it cute?" But by age three it's already indecent.

JACK (*Good-naturedly annoyed*) You insist on thinking of it as sexy.

HERB And you insist on pretending we're in a laboratory where everyone is going to be so high-minded. Look, we'll get the designer to do the set so that the bathroom is downstage . . . and there's this piece of furniture just below it . . . and he comes out just above it . . . and he's covered to just below his belly button. But we'll know he's naked, because she says, "For God's sake, put something on."

JACK You can hear a man's wife saying that?

HERB Yes.

JACK What would her motive be?

HERB She just wants him to put something on.

JACK Come on, Herb . . . you've called me often enough on motivation . . . It would mean that the thing is some kind of monstrosity frightening to the eye . . . or that she's prudish and doesn't like her husband appearing naked in

front of her. Neither of these things is true of my couple
. . . You see, Herb . . .

HERB Look, you got a lovely, sensitive play here, except for
this one moment.

JACK This one moment is what makes the whole play real
. . . Look, people go to European movies, or art movies
. . . not because of art but because of Life. They know
there's some chance that the story will break through to the
absurdities and truth of life . . . You want to know a scene
I've got in my notebooks that I've never seen? I've lived it,
but I've never seen it . . . A guy is giving a girl a snow
job. He's almost got her where he wants her . . . and the
timing is everything. He can't let a moment pass, or the
mood change, or he's lost her. It's the end of the evening,
and he's kissing her and fondling her . . . and she's smiling "yes" but telling him to run along home like a good
boy. The only trouble is that this guy is running a race with
his bladder . . . And he's finally got to go, and he's lost
it . . . Didn't that ever happen to you? (HERB *gives him a
look and turns away*) Now that's real life . . . But when
are we gonna see that scene in an American movie or in
the American theatre? I feel like going to the edge of the
stage, like Mary Martin in *Peter Pan* . . . and saying to
the audience . . . "Do you believe in life as it is lived?
. . . Don't you want to see it?" I think they want to see
the ironies, the paradoxes . . . the absurdities . . . Hell,
Life is a tragedy played by comedians. They know it. Let
them see it onstage.

HERB Look, Jack, you know more about tone than I do . . .
TONE . . . You can't shift tone like that in a play.

JACK You do it in life . . . at least in my house. One moment we're making love . . . the next minute we're wran-

gling about something . . . and then the dog gets excited and pees on the carpet . . . and we break up laughing.

HERB   That's your house! Your assumption is that what you experience in your house, they experience. I don't go around naked in my house. This is your assumption.

JACK   I would assume that at least in a man's bedroom and bathroom he goes naked occasionally. I don't walk around the living room or the kitchen, as a rule . . . I've done it a couple of times in the summer when the kids are away. It's okay . . . Gave me a feeling . . .

HERB   (*Flips on the intercom*)   Dorothy.

DOROTHY   (*Over the intercom*)   Yes, Mr. Miller?

HERB   Any actors out there?

DOROTHY   (*Over the intercom*)   Yes, Mr. Miller.

HERB   Send one in.

JACK   What's this all about?

HERB   If we're gonna get this show on the road, we're gonna have to start seeing actors.
(JACK *takes off his coat*)

DOROTHY   (*Enters from the door, left*)   Mr. Richard Pawling (*He doesn't follow at once. She calls him*) Mr. Pawling! (RICHARD PAWLING *enters. He is thirty-five. He is overeager, self-explaining, and anxious.* DOROTHY *exits*)

HERB   (*Shaking hands*)   Hello, Mr. Pawling.

PAWLING   How do you do?

HERB   This is Mr. Jack Barnstable.

PAWLING   (*Awed and pleased*)   Oh . . . (*Crosses to shake hands very appreciatively with* JACK) How do you do, Mr. Barnstable. It's a pleasure. A *real* pleasure! I . . . uh . . . didn't really expect to be seen by anyone . . . I was just bringing some new pictures of myself around for your files.

HERB   That's all right, Mr. Pawling. Please sit down.

PAWLING   Thank you . . . I've got my hair long because I'm up for a part in a Western series . . . but I can cut that . . . And the mustache is temporary . . . for a commercial. I'm a doctor, and I guess they feel it gives more dignity, you know. (*He rises*) "One out of every two doctors recommends . . ." (*He laughs nervously and sits again*) I . . . uh . . . worked for you once, Mr. Miller.

HERB   Oh?

PAWLING   About five years ago. I understudied Steiger . . .

HERB   (*Not registering at all*)   Oh, yes.

PAWLING   (*There is awkward silence, as* JACK *watches* HERB *and* HERB *waits*)   Uh . . . what kind of part is it, if I may ask?

HERB   It's a very good part . . . the lead.
(JACK *is aghast and goes to sit at one side of the room*)

PAWLING   (*Worried that he is giving the wrong impression, he follows* JACK)   I can be taller . . . I don't have my elevator shoes on . . . Or shorter. I mean . . . I can pretty well adapt. The hair is dark now, but you may remember, Mr. Miller, it was blond when I worked for you last.

HERB   Oh, yes.

PAWLING   (*Going on nervously*)   I'm pretty well tanned up because of this Western . . . I told you . . . but if I stay away from the sunlamp for a couple of days . . . I . . .

well . . . look more . . . intellectual, Mr. Barnstable . . .
if that's what you're looking for. Also, I have my contact
lenses in now, but I do have glasses, if that's closer to the
image. (*He whips his glasses out and puts them on. He is
thrown off balance by the two sets of lenses. After a moment,
he takes them off*) And, of course, I do have other clothes
. . . And my weight's variable . . . I mean, if you're looking for someone thinner.

HERB Actually, we're looking for someone rather . . . well,
someone who can look a little pathetic and ridiculous.

PAWLING (*Without a moment's hesitation*) That's me . . .
I mean, put me in the right clothes . . . a little big for
me . . . and I look like a scarecrow . . . I can shrink inside
my clothes.

HERB The question is, can you shrink inside your skin?

PAWLING (*Looks from one to the other, smiling*) I can if
I think it. If I can think it, I can be it . . . You see, here's
my composites, the pictures I was leaving with the girl.
(*Whips out a photo sheet and shows it to* HERB *at the desk*)
A doctor . . . a cowboy . . . a soldier . . . businessman
. . . small-town grocer . . . You can't notice it, probably,
but I'm wearing a hairpiece . . . I look quite different without it. Do you want me to . . .

> (*He makes a move to strip off the very obvious hair-
> piece*)

HERB No, no. You don't have any pictures of you in a bath-
ing suit, do you?

PAWLING No. I . . . uh . . . When are you planning on
doing the play?

HERB No dates yet.

Martin Balsam as RICHARD PAWLING and George Grizzard as
JACK BARNSTABLE.

PAWLING I could work out in a gym from now until then. I can put on quite a bit of muscle in a few months.

HERB That wouldn't be necessary. "Ridiculous," I said.

PAWLING Oh, yes. I forgot. Well, as I said, I *do* look ridiculous.

HERB Jack, why don't you fill Mr. Pawling in? Take over. After all, it *is* your idea.

JACK I don't think Mr. Pawling is exactly the type.

PAWLING (*Coming to* JACK) I can look a lot younger.
　　(*He "acts" younger*)

JACK It isn't that.

PAWLING Or older.
　　(*He slumps*)

HERB (*Egging* JACK *on*) I think you owe it to Mr. Pawling to go into the part and the requirements. I mean, I don't think we should jump to any conclusion as to whether he's right or wrong. Particularly in this part, with its special requirements . . . I don't see how we can know until we've really seen Mr. Pawling.

PAWLING Perhaps if I could read the script, I could come in looking more like . . . I mean, you know . . . dressed more for the part.

HERB (*Seeing that* JACK *is not going to do anything*) Well, Mr. Pawling . . . this is an unusual part. It's a husband, and . . .

PAWLING Well, I've been married three times.
　　(*He laughs nervously*)

HERB And in the opening scene, it's right after breakfast, and his wife's in bed, with the newspapers and coffee, and the husband is in the bathroom, which is adjacent to the bedroom . . . where the wife is lying in bed, having coffee, reading the papers. It's morning, you see, and she's having her morning coffee . . . and the husband is in the bathroom, and he's brushing his teeth, and the water's running . . . you know, while he's brushing his teeth . . . and she's talking to him . . . Why are you smiling?

PAWLING Well, I mean . . . that's a situation I know like the back of my hand. My wives . . . they could never get it through their heads that you can't hear when the water's running.

HERB That's his first line. He turns off the water, and he comes out and says, "Honey, you know I can't hear you when the water's running."

PAWLING Well, you've got every husband with you from then on . . . I didn't say "honey," but I remember distinctly saying "For Christ's sake, how many times do I have to tell you I can't hear you when the goddamned water's running?" (*Turns to* JACK) Excuse me, Mr. Barnstable.

JACK (*Burning*) Why did you say "excuse me" to me?

PAWLING I don't know.
(*Shrugs as if to say "Did I do something wrong?"*)

HERB So the scene is familiar to you? (PAWLING *makes a gesture—"of course"*) What did you wear when you brushed your teeth?

PAWLING (*Immediately*) I can wear anything you want.

HERB But what did you wear?

PAWLING It depends. Sometimes I sleep in my underwear . . . sometimes pajamas.

HERB   In this play the character wears nothing. He's brushing his teeth bare-assed.

PAWLING   I can do that. I've done that. Naturally. In the bathroom. Of course. Very good. Why not? The bathroom's offstage. Why not? But why is it important what the man is wearing if it's offstage?

HERB   (*Motions for* JACK *to take over*)   Uh . . . Jack.

PAWLING   I mean, excuse me, I'm not questioning it. I can see where it helps the actor to understand the character. He's the kind of guy who brushes his teeth . . . (*He looks at* JACK) in the nude. Yes. I can handle that . . . because I've done that.

HERB   He turns off the water, comes into the bedroom, and says the line you said . . . Only without the blasphemy, because Mr. Barnstable doesn't like blasphemy onstage.

PAWLING   Of course . . . I see, yes. He says the line . . .

HERB   Bare-assed. (PAWLING *looks from one to the other*) How would you feel about that? The actor has to stand there naked . . . and say the line.

JACK   (*Getting angry, realizing that* HERB *is making a test case with this nonentity*)   Look, let me explain it. This is not just for shock effect, or for thrills. There's nothing sexy about it. I just think that it's an added value for an audience to relate to a situation they know. The only shock would be the pleasurable shock of recognition . . . the honesty and truthfulness of it. The man then goes back in the bathroom, and next time we see him, he's in a bathrobe, and we never see him naked again . . . I think it can be one of the great moments in the history of the theatre . . . Like Nora slamming the door in *A Doll's House.*
    (PAWLING *has never heard of* A Doll's House)

21

HERB (*To* PAWLING) How would you feel about that?

PAWLING (*Looking from one to the other*) I have to apologize.

HERB (*Thinking he has won his point, he speaks kindly*) I understand, Mr. Pawling.
(*He turns to smile his satisfaction at* JACK)

PAWLING I've got a hole in my sock. (*He takes off his coat and tie*) I told you, I really didn't expect to see anyone. I was just dropping by to leave some new pictures . . . I didn't expect an interview. (*Goes on undressing. He takes off his shirt*) How ridiculous do you want this man to look? I mean, I'm not a ninety-eight-pound weakling, but if I didn't eat anything for a while, and if I shaved the hair on my chest . . . is this guy supposed to be funny?
(JACK *won't answer; he looks at* HERB)

HERB No, he's the leading man. It's just that Mr. Barnstable wants to puncture this idea of the muscular and hefty man. He wants, in a sense, everyman.

PAWLING (*In his undershirt*) Well, that's me . . . I'm really the original anonymous man. People are all the time coming up to me and thinking they've met me . . . I got a face looks like everybody else's. (*Pulls off his undershirt*) You see, I haven't got much muscle on my arms . . . and if I stand in a certain way, it even looks like less. (*He moves around demonstrating*) The hair on the chest . . . I can shave that off and powder it down . . . and if I stand right . . . But then, they won't see that, I suppose. If I come in from downstage and look up at her in the bed (*He acts it out, going downstage and walking up*) they'll only get a view of my tail and side . . . (*He is standing, trying this view out*) Still, we ought to have that shaved.

HERB   But you see, Mr. Pawling, you don't come in from downstage. You come in from upstage. I believe that's Mr. Barnstable's idea.

PAWLING (*Stares out at the audience full-face, gradually getting the idea of what this involves*)   Well . . .
(*He starts to take off his trousers*)

JACK (*Embarrassed*)   I think that will be all, Mr. Pawling.

PAWLING (*Sits down, slipping off his shoes so that he can get his trousers off. We see the hole in the sock*)   My chest is misleading. That hair. But you see, my legs . . . (*As he strips off his trousers*) I mean, I wouldn't want you to count me out because of that hair on my chest.

HERB (*Watching* JACK's *embarrassment*)   I think you're quite right, Mr. Pawling. Mr. Barnstable is out after a certain uncompromising effect, and I think we should see the whole works.

PAWLING (*The trousers are off; he stands there*)   Well, the legs, as you see, are . . . well . . . ridiculous.

HERB   I think you're being modest, Mr. Pawling. But you see, I don't think the legs, or the hair on the chest, or anything like that really matters . . . Because when you come out onstage absolutely skinny, nobody is going to be looking at your legs, or your chest. So the question is . . . is the rest of you ridiculous? You see, Mr. Barnstable has the interesting theory that most women look upon that part of their men as ridiculous and pathetic . . . and he wants to present his man not as a stud, not as a romanticized phallic symbol, but as the miserable, laughable thing it is. Now, Mr. Pawling?

PAWLING   Well, I . . . It's embarrassing discussing this sort of thing, but . . . girls have sometimes . . . uh . . .

laughed, or giggled . . . at first. Of course, it's not the look that counts. I mean, we all know that. (*They are all silent for a moment*) Well, I've been turned down for parts because I was too short or too tall . . . too fat or too thin . . . too young or too old . . . But I never did or didn't get a part because of . . . (*He swings his arms in embarrassment*) What the hell!
(*He starts to unbutton his shorts*)

JACK Hold it, Mr. Pawling!
(*He gathers up Pawling's clothes*)

PAWLING But I agree with you completely, Mr. Barnstable. It's time the American theatre grew up.

JACK (*Holding out his clothes to him*) Thank you for your cooperation, Mr. Pawling. You can dress in the next room. There's a door into the hall from there . . . (*Indicating the door, right*) And we'll be in touch with you.

PAWLING (*Not giving up*) But, I mean, if that's going to be the whole point of the thing . . .

JACK (*Heading for the door, left*) I'm sure that that's as adaptable as the various other parts of your body . . .

HERB But, Jack, I don't see how you're ever going to— (JACK *has turned and gone into the secretary's office, left.* PAWLING *looks after him, standing there in his shorts and socks, with his arms full of clothes*) Well, thank you, Mr. Pawling. There's not much point without Mr. Barnstable.
(*He holds the other door for* PAWLING)

PAWLING (*Crossing to follow* JACK) I didn't say anything to . . . uh . . . ? I mean . . .
(*Catching him at the left door and ushering him back across to the right door*)

HERB No. Thank you very much. And I'd keep this all very

much to myself, if I were you. We're thinking of you very seriously for the part.

PAWLING You are! Well . . . Gee . . . Thank you for seeing me. It was a great honor meeting Mr. Barnstable . . . and to see you again.
(There is a certain confusion with shaking hands with all the clothes, and saying goodbye, but finally PAW-LING is out. HERB closes the door; he looks satisfied. He goes to the other door and opens it)

HERB Ollie, Ollie, ocksin, all in free.

JACK *(Comes in, mad; he goes for his coat)* I suppose you think you've won your point.

HERB Theory is theory. Life is life.

JACK That was no test. A man taking off his clothes in front of two guys is one thing—

PAWLING *(Opens the door and steps in. He is still in shorts and socks)* Oh, Mr. Miller. Oh, excuse me.
(He holds his undershirt to his bare chest. JACK stares at him and instinctively puts his overcoat over his chest)

HERB Yes, Mr. Pawling?

PAWLING Excuse me, but I've just had an idea. I've got a Polaroid camera . . . and I'll get my agent to take some pictures of me . . . uh . . . the way you want them, and I'll send them to you.

HERB Not through the mails, please.

PAWLING I'll bring them around, then.

HERB "Attention Mr. Barnstable" . . . in a plain wrapper.

PAWLING   Right. Sorry about the holes in the socks.
(*He goes back into his room*)

JACK   (*Putting on his coat*)   You're a cruel bastard. You
know we wouldn't even think of reading that guy . . .

HERB   Where you going?

JACK   I've got to have lunch with my lawyer and accountant.

HERB   Jack, I'll tell you what I'll do for the American theatre.
What about a naked woman? Now, we put the man in bed,
and the woman in the bathroom . . . naked. The water's
running. And she's talking to him . . . And when she gets
no answer from him, she comes out of the bathroom and
says, "Did you hear what I said?" And she's naked.

JACK   And he says, "Honey, you know I can't hear you when
you're naked."
(*He starts out the same door* PAWLING *used, checks
himself, and crosses to the other door*)

HERB   (*Acting as the businessman*)   Okay, Jack. Let's quit
the kidding around. Hank wants to do this part.

JACK   (*Stops in his tracks*)   He does?

HERB   But he won't appear naked. I got an offer from Warner
Brothers to pay $300,000 on a pre-production deal *if* Hank
plays the part. Now you haven't had a hit in a while . . .
Your share of $300,000 is . . .

JACK   That's insulting, Herb. You know that?

HERB   Yeah, I know. But how about it?

JACK   (*Ranting*)   I turned down two movies could have
earned me a fortune to write this play.

HERB   True. True.

JACK   For the privilege of saying what I want to say, the way

I want to say it, in the only place I *thought* where you could still say it with some freedom.

HERB   You're right.

JACK   I mean, Herb . . . If we can't be bold in the theatre . . . where else? (*He calms down a moment.* HERB *waits*) You asked Hank if he'd play the scene as written?

HERB   No. I just took it for granted what his answer would be. Anyway, I didn't know you really meant to play it . . . as written.

JACK   He didn't say anything about the scene?

HERB   Maybe he doesn't read stage directions.

JACK   On the other hand, Hank's a pretty gutsy guy. Maybe he just assumed we'd play it as written . . . You know, you bastard, you did prove one thing to me here just now . . . we couldn't play the scene with just anybody. It would have to be someone of Hank's stature . . . He'd bring his authority onstage with him . . .

HERB   So it really comes down to whether Hank with his authority . . .

JACK   (*Comes to* HERB) Will you put it on, as written, if Hank'll play it that way?

HERB   Sure.

JACK   Okay . . . I gotta get out of here, but after lunch, I'll call Hank. Let *me* talk to him . . . let me give him the background of my thinking . . . (*Heads for the door, stops, and turns*) My God, we still got a problem.

HERB   What now?

JACK   We haven't any idea what Hank looks like naked.

HERB Well, before we sign the contract, we could invite him to the Y for a swim.
(JACK *thinks about this a second, nods in assent, and leaves*)

HERB (*Shakes his head, smiling. He reaches for the phone and dials a number*) Hello, Hank . . . Herb Miller here . . . Sorry to call you at home, but I wanted to get to you fast. I'm going ahead with the play for sure this season . . . Barnstable's crazy to have you do it . . . He just left here . . . And he may be getting in touch with you, so I thought I ought to warn you about one thing and ask for your help. He's kind of a nut about that first scene. I don't know if you read all the stage directions, but the guy is supposed to be standing there in the bedroom naked . . . Oh, you did read that? Well, Barnstable's got the crazy idea he wants it played just like that . . . Naked. What? (*He rises*) But good God, Hank. We can't do that! (*He continues to listen, consternation on his face*) The shock of recognition. (*He nods dully. The right door bursts open*)

PAWLING (*His voice is heard*) Hey, Mr. Miller. Look!
(PAWLING's *right hand can be seen on the edge of the door.* HERB *dully motions* PAWLING *to go away, and barely gives him a glance. Then suddenly he realizes what he's seen. His head jerks up, straight front; then he does a slow turn to check out what he's seen*)

PAWLING (*His voice*) I told you . . . Ridiculous!
(HERB's *eyes close, shutting out the sight of what he has seen. He is sinking to his chair as the lights go out*)
Curtain

The Footsteps of Doves

The scene is the basement of a store which sells nothing but beds, mattresses, springs, frames, and all the accouterments of the bedroom. Various beds are displayed. At one side there is the usual double bed: fifty-four inches. At another side, there are two single beds.

The SALESMAN *enters with* HARRIET *and* GEORGE. *The* SALESMAN *is a dried neuter of a man.* GEORGE *and* HARRIET *are an attractive, successful couple in their late forties. She wears a very nice suit, conservative hat and white gloves. He wears a gray flannel suit, button-down blue shirt, and brown felt hat. He has had one and one-third martinis.*

SALESMAN (*As they enter*) Downstairs here you have your better mattresses and springs. All sizes, shapes and degrees of firmness.

HARRIET (*Moves past the double bed to the twin sizes*) We're interested in the twin size.

> (GEORGE *stops at the fifty-four-inch double bed and stands and stares at it*)

SALESMAN (*Flat, not too interested*) Of course, your old classifications have broken down. Your twin used to mean thirty-six by seventy-five. Now you can get them in almost any dimension you want to suit your personal tastes. It's really just a matter of the price you want to pay, the dimensions and degree of firmness, and whether you want foam rubber or inner spring.

HARRIET (*Looking at the beds*) I understand foam rubber is hot in summer.

SALESMAN For some people . . . But then, some people are

31

naturally warmer, some are colder. (*To* GEORGE, *who has sat on the double bed*) That's your fifty-four. The twins are over here.

GEORGE   Good old fifty-four.

SALESMAN   A few people still ask for it.

GEORGE   We've slept in one for twenty-five years.
(SALESMAN *is confused. He looks to* HARRIET, *who has ignored* GEORGE—*and will continue to ignore him—elaborately*)

HARRIET   How long is this one?

SALESMAN   That's our dimple model mattress . . . Apparently the buttons create dimples . . .
(GEORGE *has propped himself against the headboard of the double bed*)

HARRIET   How long is it?

SALESMAN   That's your thirty-six by seventy-five.

HARRIET (*Sitting on the bed*)   I like a reasonably firm bed. George . . . Mr. Porter . . . likes a soft bed.

GEORGE   I'm Mr. Porter.

HARRIET   We've slept in a compromise for years, and neither one of us has been happy.

GEORGE   I've been happy.

HARRIET   George, is this long enough for you? (*He is still lying on the fifty-four-inch bed*) George!

GEORGE   What?

HARRIET   See if this would be long enough for you, please. (GEORGE *saunters over and flops down, not at all interested.*

His hat topples off) Move up a little bit. (*He squirms up*) That seems to be long enough. Are you comfortable? (GEORGE *shrugs*) We should have measured the length of the old bed.

SALESMAN If you've had it twenty-five years, it's probably seventy-five inches. (*As* HARRIET *sits on the bed*) The only way to tell is to try . . . (HARRIET *is embarrassed*) You don't have to take your shoes off . . . we have those protectors . . .

HARRIET (*Embarrassed, she starts to lie down next to* GEORGE. *She has to squeeze*) George.
    (*He moves a little. They both lie rigid, on their backs*)

GEORGE Put sides and a lid on it and bury us.

HARRIET (*Sitting up*) This is how wide?

SALESMAN That's your thirty-six. They come thirty-nine too. But of course, it's not meant to hold two people . . . except under . . . special circumstances.

GEORGE (*Gets up*) That's what I'm interested in. The special circumstances. (*He moves to the fifty-four-inch bed and sits down on it, patting it*) My mother and father had one bed, one of these . . . their whole married life. They both died in that bed.

HARRIET (*Still aloof*) Your mother first, as I remember.

SALESMAN People were smaller then.

GEORGE And more loving. Now people are detached. They dance far away from each other. They want to sleep far away from each other . . . Sure, if you want to stay apart, a fifty-four-inch is too small. But that's not the idea. The idea is to get all mixed up with each other. You've seen cats

33

sleeping together. (*He proceeds to demonstrate: cuddling his arms around his chest.* HARRIET *ignores him; she goes on reading labels and looking at ticking swatches, etc.*) Or puppies, or bears. One stirs, the other stirs . . . kind of slow and easy accommodation to each other. But they stay in a lump. For reassurance, comfort. All day you bump up against hard facts, hard edges, cold bodies. Good old fifty-four throws you up against something warm and round and soft . . . (*He looks at* HARRIET. *She looks away. He speaks to the* SALESMAN) Are you married?

SALESMAN No.

GEORGE Let me tell you about twin beds . . . I tell you, the longest distance in the world is the distance between twin beds. I don't care if it's six inches or six feet. It's psychological distance . . . In an old fifty-four, you may get into bed. You don't know what you feel like . . . Then you roll up together . . . and you know . . . In twins, you got to make up your mind all by yourself, and then cross that damned gulf and find out if your twin feels like it. And then if you get there and find out you were wrong about yourself, well, it's a lot of embarrassment retreating. Or if you find out she's not in the mood . . . it's a big rejection. But in good old fifty-four, you don't make a move until you're sure of yourself, and you can pretty well sense if she's in the mood . . . And if it still doesn't work out, what the hell, you just fall asleep, all wrapped around each other. No damage done.

HARRIET (*Elaborately ignoring him*) The price is just for the mattress?

SALESMAN Yes. In each case the box spring is available for the same price. Seventy-five dollars for the mattress . . . seventy-five for the box spring.

GEORGE Same price for the double as for the single size. Right?

SALESMAN Up to the fifty-four inches.

GEORGE I've never understood that, but I've always thought it was damned nice. Somebody with a heart working there somewhere . . .
(He shrugs, still not understanding how it happened)

SALESMAN Our prices are competitive. I say that because people often come here and pick our brains and then go buy at discount houses.

HARRIET Is this hair, kapok, cotton, or what?

SALESMAN That is your sleepwell model. Fifty percent horsehair.

HARRIET This seems very comfortable to me.

SALESMAN Actually it's the one I have at home. Only I have it in the blue ticking . . . I've slept like a top for years.

HARRIET Can you make arrangements to take the old bed away when you deliver the new?

SALESMAN No. The federal law prohibits the resale of bedding. The best thing for you to do is to give it to a charity thrift shop and take a tax deduction.

GEORGE That bed goes into the attic.

HARRIET *(Not looking at him)* There is no room in the attic.

GEORGE I will make room. You saved your wedding corsage. I can save our bed.

HARRIET *(Blazing but smiling)* I will throw out my wedding corsage . . . gladly!

GEORGE I will *not* throw out the bed!

35

HARRIET Well, there's no need to discuss that here.

SALESMAN (*He has taken this all very coolly. He sees it every day*) Do you have any idea what kind of frame or headboard you would want?

HARRIET I'd like to look at your headboards. We don't want a footboard.

GEORGE Harriet!

HARRIET (*Burning, but controlled*) What?

GEORGE I want a foot. I never said I'd do without a foot . . .
(HARRIET *is acutely embarrassed*)

SALESMAN Don't be embarrassed. We see this all the time. (*He moves to the stairs*) Perhaps you'd like to discuss this alone for a few moments. I'll be upstairs if there are any questions. It's a difficult decision. Last week a couple broke off their engagement right here. (*He starts up the stairs*) People have been known to go mad down here.
(*He exits*)

HARRIET (*Turning on* GEORGE) You're drunk.

GEORGE On two martinis at lunch. And you drank most of the second one.

HARRIET Yes, to try to prevent something like this. Stop acting like a baby.

GEORGE I am not acting like a baby.

HARRIET Well, like a damned clown, then. We had this all out, over and over again at home. We've discussed it for months.

GEORGE I've changed my mind.

HARRIET It's too late to change your mind. My mind is made

up. My God, humiliating me here in front of that man.

GEORGE   That man is of no importance to me. My marriage and my sex life are.

HARRIET   Yes. The whole store heard about your sex life in graphic detail. You painted me as a bitch who turns you down all the time, and yourself as a man very unsure of his power.

GEORGE   I did not.

HARRIET   That's the way it sounded. When it wasn't sounding like that, it was like babes in the woods, going to sleep all wrapped around each other.
(She sits on the foot of a single bed)

GEORGE   Well, that's the way we do it. You know damned well you pull my left arm up over your shoulder like a blanket. It's your damned night-night, and you couldn't sleep without it.
(He demonstrates, sitting beside her)

HARRIET   Night-night or no night-night, I haven't slept soundly in twenty years.

GEORGE   I'm fighting for our marriage, Harriet. You may not think I'm serious about it, but I am. Nietzsche said the big crises in our lives do not come with the sound of thunder and lightning, but softly like the footsteps of doves. That is not exact, but it is close enough.

HARRIET   Oh, honestly!

GEORGE   A man of forty-seven. It's a dangerous age. In a double bed he's got his wife there all the time, just the touch of her, the warmth, is exciting. After twenty-five years the image of the beloved wife is not always sexually stimulating in and of itself. But the touch always is.

37

HARRIET The image of the beloved husband is not always so stimulating either.

GEORGE I understand that. And I say we're taking a big chance. Across the room alone, a man could lie there night after night saying to himself . . . "Do I really feel like it? It's cold out there." And soon he just forgets about it more and more, and then that distance between them is like the Persian Gulf. And he finally decides he doesn't want to get his feet wet sloshing from bed to bed . . . and then they've had it. The family that lies together dies together.

HARRIET (*Trying to reason with him, appealing*) George, we've discussed this.

GEORGE We've also discussed divorce . . . Three times. But when we came up to it, we couldn't do it. And I can't do this.
(*He gestures at the twin beds*)

HARRIET Well, I've got to. My back. The doctor said . . .

GEORGE —That damned quack. *Our* doctor didn't say anything about it. But you trekked around to doctor after doctor till one told you . . . some faggot, no doubt . . . to get a single bed.

HARRIET He's a perfectly good doctor.

GEORGE He's a quack and a faggot who thinks it's disgusting for you to sleep with me anyway. What's he know about it? What are you going to do when you get up and go to the john?

HARRIET Oh, for God's sake.

GEORGE You know damned well you hurry back and snuggle up to me and say, "Oh, warm me up." You pull that old left arm over like a blanket.
(*He hugs her in demonstration*)

The Footsteps of Doves

HARRIET   George, that was all lovely. I'm not regretting any of that. Only times change. People change.

GEORGE   People change, and *go* through changes. I know. And I'm trying to be sympathetic about that. I know right now you feel kind of . . . you want to be left alone. But, Harriet, that's temporary. I know.

HARRIET   How do you know and what?

GEORGE   (*Being very considerate and delicate*)   A woman comes back later with fierce desires!

HARRIET   (*Amused*)   Who told you that?

GEORGE   I read it. The *Ladies' Home Journal.* (*Defensively*) . . . I like to know. I like to be informed . . . what's going on inside your head. It's been very helpful to me on several occasions. "Can This Marriage Be Saved?"

HARRIET   —Now, George, please. Let's stick to facts. First, my back is breaking. Second, my nerves are shattered from sleeplessness. Third, you are a morning person, and I am a night person. I like to read in bed and sleep late. You like to go right to sleep and get up early. For twenty years I have turned out the light for you, and . . . Oh, this is nonsense. We've been over it all.
(*She rises and goes to the single beds*)

GEORGE   What about a queen size or a king size?

HARRIET   We've discussed that. It won't fit in the bedroom. A fifty-four or twins along each wall is all that will fit.

GEORGE   Under the windows?

HARRIET   And drafts blowing down our necks?

GEORGE   Then let's sell the house.

HARRIET   Stop being ridiculous.

GEORGE   The house is meant to serve *our* purposes, not the other way around. That damned house. I've been breaking my ass to support it, and now it's going to separate me from my wife . . . I want a divorce!

HARRIET   All right.

GEORGE   You don't care. You don't take me seriously.

HARRIET   You have a right to say "I want a divorce" three times a day. I have a right not to take you seriously. Besides, you keep looking at it from your point of view . . . Old cuddly bears under a quilt . . . a couple of soup spoons nestled in a drawer . . . old night-night. A very romantic picture. Old ever-ready . . . Subconsciously I may be rebelling against that. I may want the space so that you'll have to make the effort, wade across the Persian Gulf. Get your feet wet . . . Not just suddenly decide you might as well since you hardly have to move to get it.

GEORGE   That's damned unfair. I have never taken you for granted. I have scrupulously concerned myself with your moods and preferences and responses . . . I could have been like some husbands who just use their wives . . . bang-bang! Thanks for the use of the hall. That's what some husbands do, in case you're interested.

HARRIET   Not in our cultural and educational bracket. I've read the articles too . . . so stop congratulating yourself.

GEORGE   You sound as though you'd had a miserable time.

HARRIET   I haven't, and you know it. Now stop acting like a martyr.

GEORGE   A martyr . . . a baby . . . a clown . . . It's lucky I have a fairly firm image of myself. It will be a miracle now if I can function at all.

HARRIET   Really . . .

GEORGE   Lying in a single bed . . . with seven feet between us. How do I feel tonight? She's lying there thinking of me as a baby, a clown, a martyr . . . and I've never given her anything more than every other man in my cultural and educational bracket gives his wife . . . Better not risk it.

HARRIET   Please decide what firmness of mattress you want. Because I would like to order and get this over with and get back to our right minds.

GEORGE   What happens six months from now when you return to combat with fierce desires? But I'm over the hill from disuse. Muscles atrophy, you know.

HARRIET   People will hear you.

GEORGE   I want people to hear me. Specifically, you!

HARRIET   I hear you.

GEORGE   You hear me, but you're not listening.

HARRIET   (*Low*)   We'll get the thirty-nine-inch width. If you insist, we'll start the nights wrapped around each other . . . and then when you've decided what's playing or *not* playing that night, you can either stay for a while or go back to your own bed.

GEORGE   *I* get the cold bed.

HARRIET   *I'll* go to the other bed. My God!

GEORGE   How long do I get to make up my mind each night? Do we set an oven timer?

HARRIET   Now, I'm going to look at headboards. You decide on the firmness you want for your mattress.

(*She moves toward another showroom*)

GEORGE   I warn you, Harriet. We are at the Rubicon.

HARRIET   I thought it was the Persian Gulf.

GEORGE   I can hear the doves!
(*But she is gone.* GEORGE, *disconsolate, walks around for a moment, looking at the beds; then picking up his hat, he gives a little kick to one of the single beds and saunters off in a different direction from the one* HARRIET *took. In a moment,* JILL *comes in. She is a swinging, charming, and disarming young woman of twenty-three dressed in a slack suit. She looks at the fifty-four-inch bed and smiles. She casually looks around the area and senses herself alone. She sits on the bed and bounces a few times. She puts down her purse, removes her jacket, leaving her dressed in sweater and slacks. She kicks off her shoes and lies down on the bed.* GEORGE *re-enters, staring off after* HARRIET, *scowling. He turns and sits on the single bed. He sees* JILL *across the way and rises in the same motion.* JILL *bounces up and down a couple of times, then turns over and lies on her stomach. She then assumes a couple of sleeping positions. She leans on one elbow and looks at the other side of the bed, as though she were looking down at another person. She smiles, as though in answer to something he had said, and gently moves a lock of hair from his imaginary face. She continues to size up the bed; then she sees* GEORGE)

GEORGE   (*Waggling a finger at her*)   Good morning. Sleep well? (JILL *sits up and smooths her sweater*) I'm sorry. I didn't mean to embarrass you.

JILL   Why didn't you cough or something?

GEORGE   To be perfectly frank, I was enjoying watching you. You seem to have a true appreciation of good old fifty-four.

JILL   Of what?

GEORGE   Good old fifty-four. The width.

JILL   Oh. Well, I've always slept in a single.

GEORGE   (*Remembering her antics on the bed*)   Oh? About to be married?

JILL   No. Just divorced.

GEORGE   Well, I don't wonder, sleeping together in a single bed.
(*He laughs at his bad joke*)

JILL   We slept together in *two* single beds.

GEORGE   I see.

JILL   "So much better when either of you gets a cold," his mother said.

GEORGE   Do you get colds?

JILL   No. His mother got the colds. I got a divorce. (*She tests the bed by striking it in some way which* GEORGE *finds mysterious*) He was a born bachelor. I think getting up and going back to his own bed gave him the comforting impression he wasn't really married.

GEORGE   This day and age, I'm surprised you didn't find that out before you were married.

JILL   That was my fault. I only had this thirty-inch bed. I couldn't very well expect him to spend the whole night in that.

GEORGE   (*Indicating the double bed*)   I take it next time you're going to know beforehand.

JILL   What I'd really like is one of those old canopy beds, with curtains, or a big brass bed. I was born in an old brass bed. Conceived in it too.

GEORGE   I think you'll find this very congenial. It has my un-
qualified endorsement. My wife and I have slept on one for
twenty-five years, and it would have held up for another ten
at least, but my wife decided it was time for single beds.

JILL   You've been married for twenty-five years?

GEORGE   Yes.

JILL   Well, men *do* keep in better shape than women.

GEORGE   (*Pulls in his gut*)   Yes . . . Well, I try to get to the
club three times a week . . . play a little squash, keep down
the old midriff.

JILL   I think men improve with age, mostly. They know
what they want and how to get it, and what to do with it
when they get it. Now, women . . . they get their men,
feather their nests, and then let themselves go. That's
cheating in my book. I'm not talking about your wife, of
course.

GEORGE   Oh, Harriet's still—

JILL   (*Going right on*)   It was all right when we were an
agrarian society and women's function was to breed children to help on the farm. But now she has a responsibility
to keep herself attractive. I wrote a paper on that in college.

GEORGE   (*Amused at her*)   I'm sure the man gave you an
A-plus.

JILL   It was a woman. She gave me a C-minus.

GEORGE   You sound very fair about the whole thing.

JILL   I should keep my mouth shut, but I think your wife is
taking a terrible risk, an attractive man like you who plays
squash.

GEORGE   Well, after all, times change. People change.

JILL   But the point is, you haven't changed. Things are very unfair in our society for men. They get these drives and urges when they're twelve or thirteen—

GEORGE   Twelve. Twelve.

JILL   And they keep them for years and years, and what are they supposed to do about them? A wider bed would be better, but I haven't the room for it.

GEORGE   One of those cookie-cutter apartments?

JILL   Never. An old brownstone. Way up at the top. A walk-up.

GEORGE   That's a curious location for a girl who admires older men.

JILL   I wouldn't be caught dead in one of those new places. The bedrooms are so gleaming and sharp and . . . antiseptic, a man wouldn't know if he was supposed to make love or operate.

GEORGE   My hopes for the younger generation are rising every minute. I lived in a brownstone once. East Fiftieth Street.

JILL   (*Fussing with swatches, not looking at him*)   I'm on East Fifty-first.

GEORGE   I had a view of the river.

JILL   I don't.

GEORGE   I was between Second and First.

JILL   I'm between Second and Third.

GEORGE   Oh, I had a friend who lived at two forty-two.

JILL   (*Matter-of-factly*)   Two twenty-six.

GEORGE   No. He was at two forty-two.

JILL   I'm at two twenty-six. (*She has been studying the mattress during this ritual of giving the address*) I like a firm mattress.

GEORGE   So do I.

JILL   Do you call this firm?

GEORGE (*Sits on the mattress and tests it*)   More or less.

JILL   How tall are you?

GEORGE   Five . . . uh . . . nine.

JILL   Weight?

GEORGE   One seventy-five . . . Stripped.
        (*He beams*)

JILL   Mmmmmmmm. Could I be a nuisance and ask you to lie down?
        (*She lies down*)

GEORGE (*He hovers over the side of the bed she's lying on, awkward*)   Of course.

JILL   What's the matter?

GEORGE   I . . . uh . . . This is usually my side of the bed.
        (JILL *squirms across to the other side.* GEORGE *looks toward the various exits for signs of* HARRIET, *and then lies down, carefully keeping away from her*)

JILL   Does this embarrass you?

GEORGE   No!

JILL   It doesn't seem to sag, does it?

GEORGE   No!

JILL   I mean, I don't roll downhill toward you?

46

GEORGE Unfortunately not.
(*A quick laugh*)

JILL How much room do you have on that side, between you and the edge? (*She hitches up and leans over him to look at and feel the distance and measure it with her hand*) Oh, quite a bit.
(*He suffers pleasantly from her hovering proximity*)

GEORGE (*Sits up*) I'm a little overweight at the moment. I should take off four or five pounds. But I haven't been able to exercise lately.

JILL Oh?

GEORGE I had an operation on my knee.

JILL Torn cartilage?

GEORGE Yes.

JILL I have a bad knee the doctor's been itching to operate on, but I don't want my knee all scarred up. It does leave a nasty scar, doesn't it?

GEORGE Well, it's not so bad.
(*He rolls up his trousers to show her his knee*)

JILL That's a very nice job he did. Anyway, scars on a man are rather attractive. I noticed you have a small scar on your upper lip. The war?

GEORGE (*Looks at* JILL *a moment*) No. My dog bit me.
(JILL *lies down again*)

GEORGE (*Still sitting up*) Of course, the proper technique in a fifty-four-inch is not to lie like two mummies, but entwined.

JILL Yes, all snuggled around each other. I'm an indiscriminate snuggler. Cats, dogs, dolls, stuffed animals, et cetera.

47

GEORGE   Are you a morning person or a night person?

JILL   What do you mean?

GEORGE   Some people are wide awake and full of vigor in the morning . . . others at night.

JILL   I guess you could say I'm a morning person . . . But I'm adaptable.

GEORGE   I'm a morning person.

JILL   *Are* you? (*Popping up*) Well, this is all daydreaming anyway. (*She starts to put on her shoes and jacket*) I can't afford a new bed yet. I'll probably have to wait till Mom and Dad die and I get the old brass one I was born in. Thank you very much. I have to be getting back to work.

GEORGE   What kind of work do you do?

JILL   I want to do something in design. But at the moment I do jobs of typing at home . . . manuscripts . . . short stories, novels . . . that sort of thing.

GEORGE   I see . . . I started a novel when I was in college.

JILL   Did you?

GEORGE   I never finished it.

JILL   That's too bad.

GEORGE   Maybe I ought to get back to it.

JILL   Well, if you want it typed, you have the address.

GEORGE   What? Oh. Oh, yes . . . two forty-two.

JILL   Two twenty-six . . . The name is Jill Hammond. (*Shaking hands*) Thank you very much for your help. Your name is—

GEORGE   Uh . . . Porter. George . . . George Porter.

JILL   Good-bye, Mr. Porter . . . Good luck with your novel. (*She smiles sweetly and leaves briskly.* GEORGE *remains at the foot of the stairs, wondering what has happened. He has a silly grin on his face*)

HARRIET (*Coming in*)   George, I've picked the headboards . . . Very simple, clean lines.

GEORGE (*Out of his reverie*)   Okay.

HARRIET   Have you chosen the mattress you want?

GEORGE (*Moving to the single bed*)   Uh . . . well, yes. This one will be fine.

HARRIET   Look, George . . .

GEORGE   Yes?

HARRIET   I would like the twin beds. But if it's going to be so earthshaking for you, if it's going to make all that difference, I'll struggle on with the old bed for a while.

GEORGE (*Looks at her a moment, genuinely touched, but also full of his new ideas*)   That's very thoughtful of you, Harriet. But I've been thinking down here, and I think you're right. This will be fine.
(*He pats one of the singles, a little desperately*)

HARRIET (*Still sitting on the fifty-four-inch mattress*)   I could get a better bed board and put it under my side so that I wouldn't—

GEORGE (*Interrupting her, eager*)   It's very generous of you, Harriet. Characteristically generous, but there's no question. You are right. These . . . these will be fine.
(*Standing between the two single beds, he pats both*)

HARRIET   It's not the end of the world, you know.

GEORGE I know. I know.

HARRIET We've had twenty-five wonderful years wrapped around each other. But we *are* older now. At least I am, and I'm perfectly willing to admit it.

GEORGE You're a good sport, Harriet.

HARRIET (*Crossing and sitting on the single bed with him*) You'll see. It will be better. I can read late, and the light won't bother you. And you can come home as late as you want from your poker nights without disturbing me.

GEORGE That's true.

HARRIET You can play to your heart's content.

GEORGE That's right.

HARRIET And we'll have good times.

GEORGE We sure will.
      (*They kiss*)

HARRIET Well, let's go give the man the order then. (*She stands*) George, if you want to keep the old bed up in the attic . . .

GEORGE No. No. There's really no room for it. I'll just shove it in the station wagon and give it to some charity.

HARRIET You should be able to get something for the brass frame.

GEORGE I'll dicker.

HARRIET (*Looking at the fifty-four-inch bed*) I'm not denying I'll miss it. (*She smiles*) If we get lonesome for it, we can sneak off to a motel like a couple of kids.
      (*They hug a moment.* HARRIET *starts for the stairs*)

GEORGE (*Takes a step toward the fifty-four-inch bed*) Goodbye, old friend. (*He moves a step toward the stairs, then turns*) Be seeing you.

(HARRIET *laughs, reaches out her hand, and they disappear up the stairs. The lights fade, but last of all on the fifty-four-inch bed*)

Curtain

I'll Be Home for Christmas

The play takes place in the living room and kitchen of a modern apartment, represented by no more than a couple of flats, one with a door. The time is early spring, in the afternoon.

CHUCK BERRINGER *is lying full length on the couch. He is about forty-five, large and brawny. At the moment, he is smoking a cigar and balancing a bottle of beer on his chest. He is listening to a record on a record player within reach on a small table near the couch. The music is a series of songs popular during World War II. At the moment, "I'll Be Seeing You" is playing. From the way he smokes and drinks and stares off into space, it is clear that* CHUCK *has something on his mind. He is deeply troubled, and the music and the cigars and beer are a response to the trouble.*

After a few moments, his wife, EDITH, *comes into the apartment. She is about forty. Her hair is up in curlers, covered by a scarf. She is wearing an attractive blouse, a sweater and slacks. She is carrying a small bag from the market. Her approach to things is direct, hearty, no nonsense. She is apparently somewhat insensitive, though this may only be her way of coping with things that frighten her to death. She hears the music, stops, and frowns. Still carrying the bag, she goes to the living room door, shoves it open, and looks in.*

EDITH Well, hello!

CHUCK Hello.

EDITH (*Looks at her watch*) Is my watch stopped or something?

CHUCK I just thought I'd come home early.

55

EDITH   Something the matter?

CHUCK   I thought this was your afternoon with the girls.

EDITH   Wednesdays. Used to be Tuesdays. Tuesday's hair
. . . and Fridays. (*Waves her hand to swish away the cigar
smoke*) Clarice is entertaining Teddy in here later on. (*She
picks up an empty beer bottle*) Go easy on the beer, huh?
We got that thing for the crippled children tonight. (CHUCK
*doesn't look at her. She looks at him for a worried moment;
she goes with the bundle to the kitchen and sets it on a
table.* CHUCK *gets up slowly, goes to the door and closes it.
He moves back to the couch and takes up his position again.*
EDITH, *puzzled and annoyed and disturbed, picks up the
phone in the kitchen; perching on the wooden stool, she
dials a number*) Hello, Milly . . . Edith . . . Hi. Tell me
something. Is Martin home? Well, Chuck's home, and I
was wondering if the office was declaring a holiday or closed
early or what? He's lying in the living room, smoking a
cigar, drinking beer, listening to a record and staring into
space . . . Some schmaltzy record he bought himself a couple of Christmases ago . . . songs from the War . . . (*In
the living room, the music switches to "I'll Walk Alone"*)
The only thing is that Chuck *doesn't* smoke cigars . . . he
doesn't drink beer, and I don't know when he last listened
to a record. No, forget I called, unless you hear something
. . . Probably just one of his moods . . . (*She mimics
broadly*) "What ever happened?" . . . "Where did it all go?"
. . . He used to scare the bejesus out of me when he started
wondering about the meaning of it all . . . I just don't listen any more . . . because I know that when he starts saying "What happened?" . . . he's really meaning "You happened." As though I were personally responsible for the
high cost of living and the menopause . . . I tell you, kiddo,
never marry a man at war with the inevitable . . . I'll let

56

you know. 'Bye. (*She hangs up. Her heartiness disappears. She comes back to the living room door and finds it shut. She hesitates a moment, then opens it. She comes in, looks at* CHUCK *a moment, then*) Did you see Clarice got a letter from Donny today? (*She gestures toward the table in the hall where the mail is left*) If we get a letter from that boy once a month . . . I know you won't hear of it, but I'd stop his allowance . . . (*She moves an ashtray near him*) Nothing happen at the office? (*He nods "No." She turns away from him. While she turns away, he takes a letter from the breast pocket of his shirt and casually stuffs it in his trouser pocket. He doesn't make any big thing of it*) You still going away tomorrow on the sales trip? (*He nods his head*) Would you pay the grocery bill before you go? I'm getting dirty looks down there . . . How long this time?

CHUCK Two weeks.

EDITH (*His far-off mood scares her. She attacks on her own level before he can start—if he had any intentions of starting*) Look, I know this is probably not the right time, but it never seems to be the right time . . .

CHUCK Couldn't it wait?

EDITH Till when? (CHUCK *shrugs*) Tonight it's "tomorrow" . . . and tomorrow, it's "tonight" . . . and then "when I come back." I'm sorry to break in on whatever's going on here, but I have to talk to you about these things. You're the father.

CHUCK (*Looks at her, puzzled by this "hook." He lifts the needle from the record*) What is it?

EDITH One of the things is all your responsibility. The other I could make all mine, and never let you in on it. But I think you ought to know about it before . . . in case you

have any opinions . . . (*Suddenly fanning the air*) You
don't smoke cigars. You don't drink beer.

CHUCK   Which thing is all my responsibility?

EDITH   I think Timmy is playing with himself. (CHUCK *takes
the cigar from his mouth*) Playing with himself.

CHUCK   I hope to God he is. If he isn't, he's a freak.

EDITH   Well, I'm sure he is. He moons around. He's losing
weight.

CHUCK   You think perhaps he's in imminent danger of going
blind or getting epilepsy?

EDITH   I think *he* might think that. He goes around sheepish,
and full of some kind of guilt. I think you should have a
talk with him.

CHUCK   To what end?

EDITH   I don't want his whole youth ruined by this stupid
guilt. I think you should talk to Timmy and tell him it's
okay.

CHUCK   Part of the reason a boy masturbates is in some kind
of revolt or aggression against his parents. And if I say "Go
ahead. It's all right with your mother and me," half the fun
would be gone.

EDITH   I think if he knew that you had done it, and it didn't
hurt you . . .

CHUCK   Oh, come on.

EDITH   Well, he looks at you like some kind of god, and he's
ashamed in your presence because he's doing something you
wouldn't do. It's a barrier between you. It's not fair, letting
him go around with this image of you as perfect.

CHUCK Somehow I question if that is the image of me prevailing in this house.

EDITH Okay. Let your son suffer.

CHUCK What do you mean, "suffer"?

EDITH Fighting this impulse in himself.

CHUCK I thought you said he wasn't fighting it.

EDITH The other morning when I was making his bed, there was—

CHUCK (*Sternly*) Edith!

EDITH I'm telling you, that attached to the mattress of the upper bunk, on the underneath side, staring down at him . . .

CHUCK A picture of a naked girl. Good.
(*He turns away*)

EDITH A cardboard sign . . . about so big, and on it he'd printed in large letters the word WILLPOWER.

CHUCK And you figured out from this . . .

EDITH Yes.

CHUCK Maybe the best thing for me to do would be just to turn the cardboard over and write ENJOY YOURSELF. How do you know this WILLPOWER doesn't apply to any number of other things? "Don't oversleep in the morning." . . . "Do your push-ups" . . . "Love your parents." You've got a dirty mind.

EDITH That's exactly the point. I don't want him to look on it as dirty. I want him to look on it as a normal, healthy part of his life.

CHUCK Edith, he may, in spite of your desire and efforts to

give it the *Good Housekeeping* seal of approval . . . he may just crave a corner of dirtiness in his life.

EDITH   Okay. So you want him to marry the first girl he sleeps with out of gratitude for saving him from the "nasty habit" . . . and that has happened.

CHUCK   I'm sure.

EDITH   Donny up there at college . . . what do you suppose he's doing? He never writes about any girls. He never writes, but when he does, no girls . . . I'll bet you he marries the first girl . . . and all because you never talked to him about this. (CHUCK *turns away*) I just want Timmy to look on it all as a natural hunger . . . and just as with our other appetites, we satisfy them as best we can . . . under the circumstances.

CHUCK   "The Loving Family" . . . Chapter Six.
       (EDITH *starts taking curlers from her hair*)

EDITH   You're always saying that you can't get close to your children. You try to have heart-to-heart talks with them about honesty and ideals and meaning . . . Try talking to Timmy about this. I can promise you, you'll have his undivided attention. (*There is no response from* CHUCK) Well, then, I'll send him to the doctor and have him do it.

CHUCK   No!

EDITH   Times have changed since the doctor gave you that lecture and scared you so that you're still something of a problem in that area.

CHUCK   I do not consider myself a problem in that area.

EDITH   You have trouble being frank.

CHUCK   For which we should all be grateful.

EDITH   We're not discussing you now. We're discussing the children. Another generation.

CHUCK I do not consider it prudish not to want to invade my son's pleasurable privacy. What do you want him to do? When he leaves the living room early some night, do you want him to say, "Good night, Mom . . . Good night, Dad. I think I'll mosey up to my room and . . ."

EDITH Honestly!

CHUCK A little mystery. A little snicker left in sex . . . please.

EDITH Then I'll have to find a book.

CHUCK No, dear God. I am the father here . . . good . . . bad . . . or indifferent. And if I feel my son needs to be wised up, I'll do it.

EDITH You could put it in the form of an anecdote. You told me that during the war, you . . .

CHUCK Thank you. I'll make my own occasion if I feel it's necessary.

EDITH I mean, I think if it's tied in with the war like that. It's something that interests him now. It might come up quite naturally. Anyone who was a soldier is a hero to him, and if he knows that heroes did it . . .

CHUCK Maybe we could persuade one of those TV shows about the war to slip it in casually . . .

EDITH All right. Your embarrassment at talking to your own sons about something vital comes out in jokes and quips. I don't think they are very funny.

CHUCK A little laughter, a little levity . . . leavening. Life is not, dear Edith, a desperate struggle and straining for the technically perfect orgasm . . . It's a laugh now and then. (EDITH *just stares at him*) Look, I have made several sweeping statements to all concerned that I think sex is

61

beautiful . . . one of the great blessings of mankind . . . in all its forms . . . as long as it involves no coercion, or injury, or pain . . . to anyone. Blessed be sex!

EDITH   You think general statements like that do any good? Time and again I give you all sorts of openings to go into some detail, and you side-step them . . . and it is your side-stepping makes them think that sex is dirty.

CHUCK   And I think it is your constant harping on the naturalness of sex that embarrasses the children. "Dear Lord, we thank you for this food which is about to be placed before us, and for the naturalness of sex . . ."

EDITH   You know what's going on in Timmy's mind? "I am doing injury to myself . . . to my future wife." You still feel guilty as hell about it, and that's why you can't talk to him about it.

CHUCK   I do not feel guilty about it. I just feel it is a private matter . . .

EDITH   You *do* have a feeling about it. If you'll remember during that period when I felt . . . well, after my operation, and I suggested to you—

CHUCK   Exactly! Like brushing my teeth or going to the john. It was for me to make that kind of decision, not you or some book you read.

EDITH   Well, it would have been better than all that mooning around and . . .

CHUCK   Mooning around and . . . longing . . . are sometimes better than meaningless . . . (*He doesn't go on*) I don't want to talk any more about it.

EDITH   Your son knows how you are about these matters . . . Did you know he came to me to buy him his first jockstrap?

CHUCK   Oh, Lord, I have failed my own son because he went to his mother for his first jockstrap! As I remember, he came to me first, and I said he didn't need one yet.

EDITH   Well, I don't want to even begin to think what damage that did to him.

CHUCK   Edie, he didn't need one.

EDITH   But he wanted one. He felt it was time to be a man. Perhaps you could have used it as a cue to discuss other sex matters with him.

CHUCK   Did you?

EDITH   No. But when he got it, he strutted around in it, and I told him how fine he looked in it . . . You were away.

CHUCK   Thank God!
        (*He puts the needle back on the record again. "I Should Care" is played*)

EDITH   We have to discuss one more thing. (*She goes to the door and closes it*) I don't want Clarice to hear us if she comes in . . . This thing of Clarice and Teddy . . . well . . . I've been keeping very close track of it . . . and I've been very honest with Clarice . . . (*She pushes the button on the recorder, stopping it*) I mean, she knows about everything I know. Of course, I still wish you would have an honest talk with her from the man's point of view.

CHUCK   Is that what we're going to start in on now?

EDITH   No. Because I know that that's impossible with you.

CHUCK   Damned right. I am not going to discuss with my daughter a man's . . . erogenous zones.

EDITH   All right. I gave that hope up a long time ago. But all I can say is, if I had known earlier in our marriage the

63

peculiar little things you like, we would have been better off.

CHUCK   What do you mean, "peculiar little things"?

EDITH   Never mind.

CHUCK   What do you mean "peculiar," for God's sake?

EDITH   Well, perhaps not "peculiar"—special.

CHUCK   Why don't you have a talk with Donny about a woman's sexual responses?

EDITH   I *did*.

CHUCK   Oh? Complete with anatomical details?

EDITH   No. But I talked to him about a woman's feelings . . . her moods and inclinations and disinclinations . . . that a woman expects to accommodate herself to the needs of a man to a great extent, but . . .

CHUCK   It sounds as though you made a woman sound like a long-suffering animal. You've probably frightened him to death that he's imposing on a woman every time he wants to make love to her. "If it's not too much to ask." You know, Edith, with all the sex educating you've done around here, I don't know how you've had time to do the housework.

EDITH   Nature abhors a vacuum. And you have created a vacuum as far as the sex education of your children is concerned.

CHUCK (*Serious*)   Edith, for God's sake . . . I have told them all I think they want to hear from me. Can't you get it through your head that it's grotesque, us talking to them about sex. Sex to them is full of spring and beauty and something old people like you and me don't experience . . . It's absurd to them that we are capable of feeling the same

64

thing they are feeling . . . And maybe we're not . . . They should feel something unique about love and sex . . . they should feel they're experiencing something unique and personal.

EDITH Nevertheless . . .

CHUCK They shouldn't be checking off their reactions on some grand universal checklist. "You know, Mom, that sensation you said I'd get? Well, I got it." . . . And "Ma, what do I do now? I pushed all the right buttons, and nothing happened."

EDITH Nevertheless, there is something we must discuss. Though, as I said before, perhaps I shouldn't mention it and just go ahead.

CHUCK If it's something you needn't mention, I'd appreciate your *not* mentioning it . . . at least today.

EDITH It would be just great with you if we never mentioned anything disagreeable or difficult.

CHUCK Is this disagreeable or difficult?

EDITH Well, it's just a fact of life, and it's not disagreeable or difficult if it's faced in a rational way.

CHUCK (*Salutes*) Request permission to leave the ship.

EDITH It's about Clarice.

CHUCK She's pregnant.

EDITH No. And I don't want her to be till she wants to be. That's the point.

CHUCK Okay. I'm hooked. What is it?

EDITH Clarice is going away to college next year. She'll be absolutely on her own, in a sense, and though we've done our best to give her standards, there will be pressures. Boys are not the same as they were in your day. They expect . . . They demand . . . from what I understand, talking with other mothers.

CHUCK Those must be very titillating kaffee klatsches.

EDITH You don't need to be sarcastic. We just exchange information we need. Don't tell me you men don't talk.

CHUCK Believe it or not, we don't. There's more reticence among men. We may tell dirty jokes, but we do not go into the sex problems of our wives and sons and daughters . . . What are you getting at, Edie?

EDITH Just that I think that Clarice needs more than information about sex now . . . I think, and please consider it quietly . . . rationally . . . I think I should take her to the doctor and arrange for . . . contraception. Now, please. Think about it, quietly.

CHUCK (Strong) I think it's a lousy idea.

EDITH You haven't thought.

CHUCK I said "I *think* it's a lousy idea." It did not require a great deal of thought.

EDITH But it does. Now, Chuck, you read. You know what's going on.

CHUCK I read. That does not necessarily mean I know what's going on . . . in real life. I don't believe those kids you read about represent any more than five percent of . . . It's just not in the instincts.

EDITH But it *is* the instincts. And now they're getting a chance.

CHUCK There are other instincts . . . of tenderness and affection. They're not good copy . . . but they are there.

66

Eileen Heckart as HARRIET and Martin Balsam as GEORGE.

EDITH   A boy is out for everything he can get.

CHUCK   But I got news for you. With a girl he loves, he sometimes hopes he doesn't get it.

EDITH   (*Puzzled by this, she goes on*)   Clarice and Teddy have been going together for a year now . . .

CHUCK   Against my better judgment.

EDITH   You will not be choosing her bedmates. She will be choosing them.

CHUCK   Them? Do you think they'll be in the plural?

EDITH   They could well be, from what I understand.

CHUCK   I wish you would stop "understanding" and look at your own daughter. Do you think she'll be a bed-hopper?

EDITH   You imply that I'm insulting her if I say she might be. But she might be . . . I think . . . I won't say this to her, but I don't think it is necessarily a bad idea for her to . . . experiment . . . to know. So that she won't be stuck with the wrong man . . . the only man. I know it's distasteful for you to imagine your little girl in the arms of any man, let alone several . . .

CHUCK   Oh, come on.

EDITH   I knew I shouldn't have discussed it with you. You get so emotional about it.

CHUCK   There *are* emotions involved, you know. I mean, it isn't all a chart of erogenous zones. Don't settle for a four-zone man, honey, keep looking for a six-zone man.

EDITH   But I don't want her to be trapped, pregnant by some boy she doesn't even like.

CHUCK   (*Patiently*)   I am trusting that her judgment, her emotions, will not let her get pregnant "by some boy she doesn't even like." If we haven't taught her that much in the way of standards . . .

EDITH But you can't tell. Some night some boy might get her to drink too much. I've asked you repeatedly to teach her something about that, but again, "No." You—

CHUCK (*Angry*) When's the last time, if ever, they caught us necking on this couch?

EDITH What?

CHUCK When's the last time we necked on this couch?

EDITH Once a year you bring up this necking on the couch business . . .

CHUCK When is the last time?

EDITH We got the bed, for God's sake. Why the hell should we neck on the couch?

CHUCK That's the demonstration we should give them. Necking on the couch. Kissing.
(*He turns away*)

EDITH We haven't much time before she comes in from school. And you leave tomorrow.

CHUCK Have you talked to her about this?

EDITH Not yet.

CHUCK No doctor is going to go along with you.

EDITH Not that fossil Higgins. But some doctor who knows the score certainly will.

CHUCK The pill isn't proved yet. There are possible side effects . . . and . . . my God, I forbid it!

EDITH   There's not just the pill. After all, we never used the pill . . .

CHUCK   But Clarice is a virgin. And as I understand it, a virgin can't be . . . can't use . . .

EDITH (*Cutting in*)   She is *not* a virgin.

CHUCK   How do you know?

EDITH   The doctor told me. He thought I should know.

CHUCK (*Frowns and thinks*)   Well, that doesn't necessarily mean . . . She's an active girl . . . sports . . . (EDITH *just stares him down*) Well, it doesn't necessarily mean anything. Did you talk to her about it?

EDITH   No.

CHUCK   Did *he* talk to her about it?

EDITH   No.

CHUCK   Holy Christ, I hope it wasn't that Teddy.

EDITH   You see, it's impossible to discuss this with you without your getting emotional.

CHUCK (*Accusing*)   I said I never wanted them left alone in the house . . .

EDITH   Teddy drives a car.

CHUCK   They shouldn't let kids that age drive.

EDITH   Now calm down. Stop living in the olden days. At least now you may see the point of my wanting her . . . prepared.

CHUCK (*Angry*)   It is your job to prepare her up here . . . (*He points to his head*) with a little less emphasis on the technical aspects of screwing.

EDITH   That's a charming word . . . I have tried to prepare her up here, but I am not going to be an ostrich about it.

CHUCK   Going through this . . . it's like inviting her to . . . (*He doesn't go on*)

EDITH   Her own body is inviting her. Her instincts are inviting her. Or did you want her to be a virgin when she married?

CHUCK   It is not what I want her to be, but what she wants to be. Has she asked for your help in this department?

EDITH   No, but she may be embarrassed.

CHUCK   Thank God for that. I should think you'd be embarrassed to mention it to her at this point.

EDITH   Didn't you talk to Donny about contraceptives when he went away to college?

CHUCK   Yes.

EDITH   Then why can't I discuss this with Clarice?

CHUCK   There is nothing wrong with discussing it. That is not what you suggested. Anyway, talking to Donny was another thing. It's a boy's . . . a man's responsibility. He should be prepared to handle it.

EDITH   And suppose he isn't?

CHUCK   Edith, I may not want to discuss a man's sexual attitudes with Clarice, but I don't mind discussing them with you. If a boy is out on a date with a girl, and suddenly the whole thing becomes . . . passionate . . . he does not like to hear from the girl . . . no matter how modern he is, no matter how many books on the subject he's read . . . "Go ahead, honey. It's all right. I'm prepared." If she said that, I'll tell you what goes through his head at that moment . . .

"Does this mean she does this with all the boys? . . . Does it mean she took me for granted? . . . Does it mean if I hadn't made a pass, she would have thought me a shmo?"

EDITH What is your solution?

CHUCK The man makes the arrangements . . . at least the first time.

EDITH You mean they stop while he goes hunting for a corner drugstore?

CHUCK Well . . .

EDITH Or does he just happen to have one . . . or an economy-size dozen, in his pocket? In which case, what does the girl think?

CHUCK It's different. I can't explain why. But there's a nicety in it someplace . . .

EDITH And what happens if they can't find a drugstore open . . . as we couldn't, if you'll remember . . . and the moment is possibly lost. You weren't prepared.

CHUCK I was.

EDITH We drove all over the damn countryside looking for a drugstore that was open.

CHUCK I had something in my wallet. Only by the time we got to the point, I loved you so much . . . I didn't want you to think I was the kind of guy who carried them around in his pocket . . . just in case.

EDITH Well, that's very touching. Nowadays I think the girl would think you were a fink not to be prepared, after getting her all worked up.

CHUCK I would think the girl might be flattered. To me, there is something sordid, at that moment, that beautiful

71

moment, for the guy to go fishing in his wallet for some scruffy little paper packet he'd had hidden there for weeks.

EDITH It would be a hell of a lot better than the ludicrous sight of you trying to keep me interested and at the same time driving around the countryside looking for an all-night drugstore . . . and not finding one. And you had something with you all the time!

CHUCK I shouldn't have told you.

EDITH Did you think I'd be shocked that you were prepared? My God, all girls don't have bashful fathers like you . . . I had a bashful mother who advised me to save my first kiss for the man I married . . . But not my father. He'd wised me up on what to expect . . . in very explicit terms.

CHUCK I'm sorry if I disappointed your expectations.

EDITH I don't know what your idea was, trying to appear so innocent that night. I knew there were other girls before me . . . that little romantic episode with that girl in London during the war . . .

CHUCK The idea was the way I felt about you! Were you consulting with your father during those early days of our marriage? "What do I do now, Dad? I'm involved with an amateur who's still fumbling along by his instincts."

EDITH Don't knock my dad. He opened my eyes to a great deal about life and love and the nature of man. With Mother's "disorders" he had a woman on the side. And he told me about it quite frankly . . . about the needs of a man, et cetera . . . He thought I should know this . . . And I'm damned glad he told me.

CHUCK (*After a long moment of thinking this out*) You sound as though his teaching you this . . . this matter of man's nature . . . woman on the side . . . infidelity . . . had stood you in good stead.

EDITH Well, we're not discussing that.

CHUCK I am . . . That's the goddamndest thing I've ever heard. Do you think I haven't been faithful to you?

EDITH It's not worth discussing. It's not important.

CHUCK Not important?

EDITH It's only important *not* to discuss it . . . I think.

CHUCK You have assumed bravely, stoically, armed with your daddy's sweeping wisdom about these matters, that I have been unfaithful to you?

EDITH I find it embarrassing to discuss—

CHUCK —I find it impossible not to discuss.

EDITH I'm not making any accusations.

CHUCK You are implying very heavily, and you seem to be decking yourself with some kind of sweet tolerance which I find disgusting . . . If you think I've been unfaithful to you, I'm appalled, frankly appalled, that you haven't stood up and shouted.

EDITH That would be pretty ridiculous, wouldn't it? After all, what does it matter?

CHUCK When? Please tell me when?

EDITH You're away a great deal.

CHUCK When?

EDITH Long trips, extended periods. A woman would be foolish not to expect something to happen . . . Oh, meaningless, of course . . . But I'm trying to tell you, it doesn't matter.

CHUCK Well, I'm sorry as hell to disappoint you, but there have been no little meaningless sexual skirmishes . . . My life is full enough of meaninglessness not to go looking for it in outlying districts.

EDITH You don't have to defend yourself. Nobody is making any accusations.

CHUCK You are making accusations. And you are infuriating me by your noble tolerance over something that has not taken place. And if it had taken place, I would expect you as a loving wife to stand up and howl.

EDITH Difficult as it is for you to grasp, your virginity was not a concern of mine before we were married, and your strict fidelity is not a concern of mine now. I am not your jailer, and I am not stupid. The subject is closed as far as I am concerned.
    (*She starts for the door*)

CHUCK (*Heads her off and grabs her*) Jesus Christ, men are not all like your father. All men do not relish meaningless rolls in the hay, in their own beds or other beds.

EDITH (*Moves away from him, back into the room*) We were discussing the children.

CHUCK I feel like clobbering you for assuming that I've laid every broad in every small town I've visited, all because your father gave you the lowdown. Why didn't he let you find out for yourself what your man . . . your husband would do? Because if it doesn't matter to you, it matters to me . . . It's hard as hell trying to keep any meaning going, but here, here in the most personal and private core of me,

I insist that there be meaning, I want there to be meaning
. . . I long for there to be meaning.

CLARICE (*Offstage*)   Hello.

EDITH (*Moving from* CHUCK, *calling out*)   Hello, dear.

CLARICE (*Enters. She is eighteen and lovely. Her arms are
full of schoolbooks. She comes into the living room*)   Hi.
(*She sees* CHUCK *and looks surprised*) Hi . . . Surprise.

CHUCK (*As she comes to him, recovering from his anguish*)
Hi, baby.
(*They embrace a second*)

EDITH   I'll get the room aired out and cleaned for you and
Teddy. Did you see you have a letter from Donny?

CLARICE   No . . .
(*She leaves and heads for the kitchen.* EDITH *has been
gathering her purse, hair curlers, and various items*)

CHUCK (*Closing the door after* CLARICE)   Edith! (EDITH
stops) I forbid this, Edith. There may not be many areas in
my life where I can still act effectively, but here I can . . .
and I forbid it.

EDITH (*Moves past him to the door*)   We'll talk about it
again.

CHUCK   Don't you do anything while I'm away . . . Do you
understand?

EDITH (*After a moment*)   All right. But I wish to God you'd
join the twentieth century.
(*She starts to open the door*)

CHUCK   When Timmy comes in, send him to me, and I'll set
his mind to rest about . . .
(EDITH *opens the door and leaves, closing the door*

after her. She stands for a moment in the shadows between the kitchen and the living room)

CHUCK *(Slowly returns to the couch and sits, saddened by the scene he has just had. Then he shifts his mood slightly)* You see, Timmy . . . many good men and true do that . . . soldiers, sailors, men at war . . . men on long trips into the Arctic . . . and other places. And, Timmy, there's nothing wrong with it . . . except it's awfully lonely.
(He has said this last very simply. He turns and lies down on the couch, starts the record, and during the following, takes the letter from his pocket and rereads it)

EDITH *(Now coming into the kitchen, where* CLARICE *has been looking at her letter)* What does Donny say?

CLARICE Is that what you and Dad were talking about in there? Why he's home so early?

EDITH What?

CLARICE Donny's letter to Dad.

EDITH What letter?

CLARICE *(Reads)* "Dear Sis: Just so's you'll know what's going on. Here's a copy of a letter I've sent to Dad at his office. I'm sorry as hell to write like this, but I had to. It's cowardly to write and not face up to him on it, but we've never been able to talk . . ."

EDITH What is this?

CLARICE He didn't mention it?
(Nodding toward CHUCK*)*

EDITH What *is* it?

CLARICE I haven't finished it yet, but Donny's leaving college.

EDITH What?

CLARICE (*Reads from Donny's letter*) "I'm leaving college, Dad. I don't know what I'll do, but this is all senseless to me. This and the kind of life it seems to be leading to. I don't know yet what I want to do with my life, and I'm not going to find out here. I think you've been preparing me for the only kind of life you know. Your kind of life. I don't want to hurt you, Dad, because you've always been a good Joe to me . . . but I could never take that kind of life. The life of your generation. You all fought a war. Nobody can take that away from you . . . But after that, what happened? (*She is finding the letter more difficult and painful to read*) Whatever it was, it scares me, and I don't want it to happen to me . . . Sometimes I don't know how you do it, Dad . . . Sometimes . . . (*She falters as her eye reads ahead, then*) Sometimes I don't know how you have the courage to get up in the morning."

EDITH (*After a moment*) He wrote that to your father?

CLARICE (*Saddened and disturbed by the letter*) I guess so. (*She hands it over to* EDITH)

EDITH (*Looks at it a moment; then more in sympathy with* CHUCK *than anger at Donny*) Your father gets up in the morning . . . so that he can send your brother to a fine college so that he can write insulting letters like this.
     (*She turns toward the living room and moves into the shadows by the door, her concern for* CHUCK *clearly showing on her face*)

CHUCK (*He has finished rereading the letter. Suddenly he*

starts to sing with the record) "I'll be home for Christmas
. . . if only in my—"
      *(His voice breaks. He closes his eyes. The record
finishes and the lights dim)*
              Curtain

I'm Herbert

A very old man is sitting in one of two rocking chairs on a side porch. It is summer. He is bird-watching, his binoculars to his eyes.

HERBERT   Baltimore oriole. (*He shifts his glasses, scanning*) Bobolink. (*Shifts again*) Rose-breasted grosbeak. (*Shifts again and gets a little excited*) A black-billed cuckoo. (*He speaks louder, to someone offstage*) Grace, I saw a black-billed cuckoo.

MURIEL   (*A very old woman, dressed with faded elegance, comes onstage carrying a rose*)   My name is Muriel, foolish old man.
   (*She sits in the other rocker*)

HERBERT   I know your name is Muriel. That's what I called you.

MURIEL   You called me Grace. Grace was your first wife.

HERBERT   I called you Muriel. You're just hard of hearing and won't admit it . . . Grace . . . Grace . . . That's what I said!

MURIEL   There! You said it.

HERBERT   What?

MURIEL   Grace . . . You called me Grace.

HERBERT   Silly old woman. You call me Harry. But I call you Grace.

MURIEL   Can't you hear yourself?

HERBERT   What?

MURIEL   I said can't you hear yourself?

HERBERT   Of course I can hear myself. It's you that can't hear. I say you call me Harry. Sometimes. Your second husband . . . and sometimes George . . . your first.

MURIEL   I never did. You're saying that because you call me Grace . . . and once in a while Mary.

HERBERT   You just don't hear.

MURIEL   What's my name?

HERBERT   Silly question . . . Muriel. You're Muriel . . . Grace was my first wife. Mary was . . . way long ago.

MURIEL   Mary was before Grace.

HERBERT   No she wasn't.

MURIEL   She was.

HERBERT   I should know who was my first wife, God damn it, woman.

MURIEL   That's safe. Just call me "woman" . . . We won't get confused. It's not very flattering, but it's better than being called the names of your other wives. My name's Muriel. Your name's Harry.

HERBERT   Did you hear? You called me Harry. Pot calling the kettle black.

MURIEL   You got me confused, that's all. You always could mix me up. Back then when we were going to Europe . . .

HERBERT   We never been to Europe. That was Harry.

MURIEL   You and I went to Europe.

HERBERT   We did not. Grace and I went to Europe on our honeymoon. That's when I had money, before women had taken it all.

82

MURIEL   I've been to Europe with you.

HERBERT   You and Harry went to Europe.

MURIEL   I went to Europe with George, too.

HERBERT   Yes. Well, I'm Herbert.

MURIEL   We never been to Europe?

HERBERT   Singly, not together.

MURIEL   I think we have. You've forgotten.

HERBERT   I've got a perfectly good memory.

MURIEL   You can't even remember my name. (HERBERT
looks at her and blinks) You and I were in Venice together.
You're ashamed to remember it because of the scandalous
good times we had. You loved me then.

HERBERT   I didn't love you when you were in Venice having
a scandalous good time with whichever one it was . . .
George or Harry. Which was it?

MURIEL   It was you.

HERBERT   I've never been to Venice in my life.

MURIEL   Yesterday you said you'd never been to Chicago
. . . and I proved you wrong on that. Your second daughter by your first wife died there. We went to the funeral.

HERBERT   Grace?

MURIEL   The daughter's name?

HERBERT   No. Grace's girl.

MURIEL   Grace wasn't your first wife. Mary was.

HERBERT   Were you there? . . . I tell you, one was enough.
Two was more than plenty. I don't know what got into me
to try it a third time.

83

MURIEL   You were sick and you were too tight to hire a nurse, so you married me.

HERBERT   I got well. Why didn't I kick you out? (MURIEL *starts to cry*) Now don't cry. You know I don't mean it. You were always crying. Cried buckets at our son's wedding. Took on something awful.

MURIEL   We didn't have any children. And I don't cry. That was Mary. I'm Muriel.

HERBERT   It's no wonder I'm confused . . . which I'm not. But you all the time saying "Grace . . . Mary . . . Muriel."

MURIEL   I'm just trying to straighten you out.

HERBERT   What difference does it make? I answer when you call me Bernie.

MURIEL   I never called you Bernie. I maybe once or twice called you Harry, when I woke up sudden like and didn't know where I was. But I never knew a Bernie.

HERBERT   Bernie.

MURIEL   Never heard of him.

HERBERT   He'd be pleased to hear that.

MURIEL   Who was he?

HERBERT   You were carrying on with him when I met you.

MURIEL   I was married to Harry when you met me.

HERBERT   And carrying on with Bernie. But he cleared out.

MURIEL   That must have been Grace.

HERBERT   You were carrying on with?

MURIEL   No. Grace must have been carrying on with Bernie.

HERBERT Grace wasn't married before. I was her first.

MURIEL Not married . . . carrying on.

HERBERT She was married to Harry and carrying on with Bernie.

MURIEL You said she wasn't married before.

HERBERT *You* were. *You* were.

MURIEL What day of the week is it?

HERBERT What's that got to do with it?

MURIEL You can't remember anything any more. Senile old man. Bernie Walters!

HERBERT That's him.

MURIEL Who?

HERBERT Bernie Walters.

MURIEL I never heard of him.

HERBERT You just said his name.

MURIEL You've been saying it here for an hour. I just repeated it.

HERBERT You said "Bernie Walters."

MURIEL I said I never heard of him, and besides I wasn't married to Harry when I met you. It was George. If I'd been married to Harry, I wouldn't have looked at you. Fine, strapping man . . . may he rest in peace. Oh, what he did in Venice!

HERBERT You see, it was Harry in Venice.

MURIEL Of course it was Harry in Venice.

HERBERT You said it was me.

MURIEL   You? Huh? You wouldn't have it in you to do a thing like that.

HERBERT   What? A thing like what?

MURIEL   (*Laughs*)   Don't be jealous of a dead man. I've done my best to forget him, George, like I promised when I married you.

HERBERT   I'm Herbert.

MURIEL   Do you keep repeating it so you won't forget who you are?

HERBERT   You called me George just now.

MURIEL   A hearing aid's a cheap thing . . .

HERBERT   See here, Grace . . .

MURIEL   I'm Muriel.

HERBERT   You talk about me . . . What about you? "Muriel. I'm Muriel."

MURIEL   Cuckoo!

HERBERT   (*He takes up his binoculars*)   Where? I wouldn't call you Grace. Grace was soft and gentle and kind.

MURIEL   Why'd you leave her then?

HERBERT   I didn't. She died.

MURIEL   Mary died. Your first wife. You got sick of Grace and left her and married me.

HERBERT   Left Grace for you?

MURIEL   Yes, you silly old man.

HERBERT   All wrong. Grace was my darling.

MURIEL   She drove you crazy.

86

HERBERT   My first love.

MURIEL   Mary.

HERBERT   Mary drove me crazy.

MURIEL   She was your first love. You've told me about it often enough. The two of you young colts prancing around in the nude.

HERBERT   Mary?

MURIEL   Yes.

HERBERT   I never saw Mary naked. That was her trouble. Cold woman.

MURIEL   That was Grace.

HERBERT   Grace I saw naked. Oh, how naked! There was never anyone nakeder.

MURIEL   You can only be naked. You can't be more or less naked.

HERBERT   You didn't know Grace.

MURIEL   Mary. I did know Grace.

HERBERT   Naked?

MURIEL   Keep a civil tongue in your head.

HERBERT   I never saw you naked.

MURIEL   No, and not likely to. What'd be the point? You couldn't do anything about it.

HERBERT   Oh, that's what you think.

MURIEL   You married me at seventy . . . and you were through then . . . Except for dreaming.

HERBERT You're lying. We had some good go's together, down by the beach.

MURIEL You and I were never near a beach. And you were never near me in that way.

HERBERT Old women forget . . . forget the joys of the flesh. Why is that?

MURIEL I don't forget Bernie.

HERBERT Who?

MURIEL Bernie Walters.

HERBERT Never heard of him.

MURIEL My second husband. I was married to him when Harry came along . . . But Harry went away and then you came along . . . a long time after. Platonic marriage. That's what we've had, you and I, George. But it's all right.

HERBERT Platonic under the willow tree that June?

MURIEL What willow tree?

HERBERT Oh, I've been good to you, Mary, for all your carping and your falling off in your old age, because I remember that willow tree. Muriel never knew about it. We were wicked.

MURIEL If I thought you knew what you were talking about, I'd get mad. But I know you're just babbling. Babbling Bernie . . . That's you. Herbert used to say "How can you listen to him babble?"

HERBERT I'm Herbert.

MURIEL If it makes you feel more secure. Go on. Keep reminding yourself.

HERBERT You called me Bernie.

MURIEL   Oh, sure, sure. And you've never been to Chicago.

HERBERT   I have so. I went there when my daughter died.

MURIEL   Well, I'm glad you admit it.

HERBERT   Why shouldn't I admit it? It's so. You just try to confuse me . . . Bernie, Harry, George, Grace, Mary.

MURIEL   You started a long time ago, slipping. Only then you were more honest about it. Very touching. When we went to Florida and you gave me the tickets and said, "Grace, my mind's slipping, take care of the tickets."

HERBERT   Your name's Muriel.

MURIEL   Yes, yes, lovey. My name's Muriel.

HERBERT   You referred to yourself as "Grace."

MURIEL   (*Sarcastic*)   Oh, very likely. Very likely.

HERBERT   You said I gave you the tickets to Florida and said, "Grace, my mind's slipping."

MURIEL   Well, it was.

HERBERT   I've never been to Florida.

MURIEL   Ho-ho. Well, let's not go into it. The pongee suit.

HERBERT   I never owned a pongee suit.

MURIEL   You said it was the same suit you wore when you married Helen, and we had a long discussion about how ironic it was that you were wearing the same suit to run away with me.

HERBERT   Who's Helen?

MURIEL   You were married to her, silly.

HERBERT   I was running away to Florida with you and I was

so old my mind was slipping and I couldn't remember the tickets?

MURIEL   Lovey, you're running a lot of things that happened at different times together now. Maybe you should just sit quietly for a while, Harry, till you get straightened out.

HERBERT   My name is Herbert.

MURIEL   That's right. We'll start from there. You're Herbert and I'm Grace.

HERBERT   You're Muriel.

MURIEL   That's right. Now let's just leave it at that now, or you won't sleep tonight.

HERBERT   I always sleep.

MURIEL   A fortune for sleeping pills.

HERBERT   I never had one in my life.

MURIEL   And you've never been to Chicago either, I suppose.

HERBERT   Never. Why should I have gone to Chicago?

MURIEL   Only because our daughter died there and we went to the funeral.

HERBERT   We had no children together.

MURIEL   I think we shouldn't talk any more now. You're getting confused.

HERBERT   You never let me near your lily-white body.

MURIEL   Ho-ho . . . and what about that afternoon under the willow tree? I think that's when we conceived Ralph.

HERBERT   Who is Ralph?

MURIEL   Ralph is your stepson. Good God!

HERBERT   I conceived my stepson under the willow tree?

MURIEL   I'd prefer it if we just remained quiet for a while. You can't follow a train of thought for more than a moment . . . and it's very tiring trying to jump back and forth with you. Just close your eyes and rest . . . Are your eyes hurting you?

HERBERT   No.

MURIEL   That medicine must be very good then.

HERBERT   What medicine?

MURIEL   You see, that's what I mean.

HERBERT   I never had any medicine for my eyes.

MURIEL   Yes, all right. All right. Let's not argue, George.

HERBERT   I'm Harry.

MURIEL   Yes, yes. All right. We'll just hold hands here, and try to doze a little . . . and think of happier days . . .
     (*She takes his hand and they close their eyes and rock*)

HERBERT (*After a long moment*)   Mmmmm . . . Venice.

MURIEL (*Dreamy*)   Yes . . . Oh, yes . . . Wasn't that lovely . . . Oh, you were so gallant . . . if slightly shocking . . .
     (*She laughs, remembering*)

HERBERT   The beach . . .

MURIEL   The willow tree . . .

HERBERT (*Smiling*)   You running around naked . . . Oh, lovely . . . lovely . . .

MURIEL   Yes . . . lovely . . .
   (*They go on rocking and smiling, holding hands as the lights dim*)

Curtain